Out The Clara Road

The Offaly Anthology

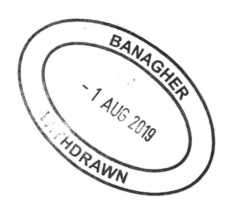

edited by Rita Ann Higgins

Offaly County Council

Joe Kenny

The Sunshine Days

It was more than a shock, it was a bombshell, and I refused to believe it. 'The Smiler' above all people. It just wasn't on. Not that 'The Smiler' was a saint, or pretended to be. Far from it. But a thief - no way. The whole thing was crazy. I just couldn't believe it at all.

If I say it all began in 'The Kremlin' I'm not talking about the dreaded citadel of the Russian Communist Party, although no doubt the name derived from there and while our Kremlin was neither feared nor hated, I suppose some people felt that it had about it a certain air of mystery, and perhaps, that prompted the nickname. Still, if ever there was a misnomer, this was it, for we saw no sinister aspect to what was a strange but rather benign assembly, a centre of banter and cross-talk, mostly good-natured. Maybe whoever christened it was trying to suggest the social importance of the place for those who frequented it. I look back now as one who having, at some expense, received a prolonged formal education in many respected establishments, acquired in 'The Kremlin' a considerable quota of informal education from its resident sages and the visiting philosophers as well as from the assortment of vagrants, teachers, merchant seamen and men of much, little or no property who crossed the threshold from time to time.

I have many happy memories of 'The Kremlin', vivid memories, happy memories. It was part of the sunshine days we all remember from our youth. But I find it hard to describe the place or the people. It is not easy to conjure up the atmosphere and it would require the verbal skill of a Charles Dickens or a Con Houlihan to give its real flavour in words. 'The Kremlin' was a social centre before that term was invented and it had a vibrancy and an enchantment that no formal institution could possess. As far back as I can recall, the premises was a gathering place for local men, a place where people dropped in at will and stayed and felt free to do so. The house belonged to two bachelor brothers of middle age, Pat and Larry Regan, and it had at the front a large shop window, originally with removable wooden shutters. When the shutters were removed, the men could sit on the window sill. In rural areas, bachelor houses tended to become rambling houses and maybe the absence of a female presence was one of the reasons why Regan's became a gathering place. Its location too was crucial. In a war situation, it would have had considerable strategic importance. The view from the front door covered the length of the town from Moran's in Upper Clare Street to Smith's in Main Street - over half a mile. The verbal snipers who congregated at Regan's appreciated this scope of vision and the number of targets that could be covered at one time. Almost everything that moved in the town was within range. In a pre-television age, Regan's front door was multichannel land.

It was in these premises, already a gathering place for men, that Sonny Waldron set up his shoe repair workshop after the war. Sonny, in his forties, had mended shoes at his home outside the town for many years. At school a neighbour of his had told me about him. Sonny was a man of quick and lively intellect. He had a great interest in history and in books. He could quote verbatim stanza after stanza of song and recitation and often while stitching would declaim in full 'The Cremation of Sam McGee' or excerpts from Robert Emmet's speech from the dock. These things apart, his abiding passion was Gaelic football. He was Chairman of the local football club and on his arrival there Regan's became the unofficial GAA headquarters in the town.

Sonny was the presiding genius of 'The Kremlin' and the brothers, Pat and Larry were the background figures who quietly or often in Pat's case, not so quietly, saw to it that certain standards of behaviour and propriety were not transgressed. But without doubt the star turn in the place was 'The Smiler' Moriarty. 'The Smiler' worked in the bank and if you saw him poring over the vast ledgers of that time in his place of work, looking like a respectable clerk in a Victorian office, you would get no indication of the quicksilver wit, the fiendish spark of roguery, the complete disregard for the opinion of hog, dog or devil that reposed behind his timid spectacles.

He came from Kerry and while his poor eyesight kept him sidelined, he regaled us at length with stories of his Kerry heroes, Billy Myers, Danno

Keefe and Jackie Lyne and this gained him immense respect and credibility in our circle. He was a singer too, with songs that were new to us, songs that delighted us all and no one more than Sonny. So, it transpired that 'The Smiler', because of his lack of involvement on the playing field and his banking background, was appointed Treasurer of the football club.

'The Kremlin' however was not just a football forum. All topics were discussed there with wit and humour, often seriously but never solemnly. Of course, in modern terms, the place was a bastion of male chauvinism. But when ladies entered, as they did regularly in the course of Sonny's business, they were treated with courtesy and civility. In one way, 'The Kremlin' was the epitome of equality of the sexes and of equality of esteem for all classes, high and low, in as much as when varying degrees of character assassination were being indulged in, there was never any discrimination on the grounds of gender, creed or social standing. Everybody was a legitimate target.

In the workshop at the front, where Sonny plied his trade, there were no seats. You either sat on the counter or stood. In winter, heat was provided by a paraffin stove which stood where Sonny worked. The whole place was rather ramshackle. Sometimes you wondered if anything other than cobwebs held the walls and sagging ceiling together.

Behind the workshop, there was a kitchen. Here the decor was slightly better but must and dry rot were evident everywhere. What lay above the rickety stairs I had no desire to learn. That area was out of bounds to all save Larry and Pat.

The bachelor brothers participated fully in all that went on in the workshop at the front where access was open to all. In the kitchen another group congregated, usually in the evening. This was a more select group. Some people held dual membership but admission to the inner sanctum was not open to all. It was acquired or bestowed after a strict process of selection and invitation. In a way, the kitchen area corresponded to the House of Lords and to be installed there was a privilege.

As a gathering place, 'The Kremlin' was more a day-house than a night-house. At any hour of the day there were always a few there, but it was never a late night haunt. I suppose we were sort of indoor corner boys and we kept corner boys' hours. The House of Lords sat late on occasions, but never after midnight.

All this came back to me in a Midland town years later. I had lost touch with 'The Kremlin', the town and the people. No family remained to bring me back there, or to keep me informed of events. I had spent some time working in the Third World and having fulfilled my contract there, I came back to Dublin and set up a small consultancy business. A particular assignment had brought me to the Midlands and I was staying overnight in the local hotel. There in the bar I met a man who had been a regular in 'The Kremlin' so many years before. He was a Land Commission Inspector called Breen who had later taken up a posting in the Midlands. Despite this passage of years, we recognised one another. We had a few drinks and a lot of talk. Of course, the talk tended toward reminiscence and reminiscence tended toward 'The Kremlin' and its denizens and Sonny and 'The Smiler'. And so it was from Breen that I heard something of which he thought I would have been aware. Taken aback by my surprised reaction when he first mentioned it, he told me the story. There had been serious misappropriation of funds in the GAA club over many years. Then came suspicion, allegation, accusation and public disgrace. 'The Smiler', long-term Treasurer of the club, had fallen ill and somebody had to take over the purse strings. By today's standards the sum of money was not great but over the years it came to a sizeable amount. Income and Expenditure Accounts were a foreign game to us in those days and nobody had ever asked a question. 'The Smiler' was not a man of expensive tastes, though he was, as they say, fond of a drink. I would not have been drinking at that time but I know now that each night, after the banter of 'The Kremlin' was finished, 'The Smiler' and others adjourned to the pub across the street. Maybe 'The Smiler' acted the Big Spender. Maybe Sonny got suspicious. As Breen told it, it was Sonny who got the account books checked out and it was Sonny who insisted that nothing would be hushed up. Not that the Gardai were brought in. That wouldn't be Sonny's way of doing things. There was no court case. 'The Kremlin' dealt with things in its own way and, for once, I saw that the place had been well christened. The bank too dealt with things in its own way. Again, no court case. They were not at any financial loss. But 'The Smiler' got the bullet. There was no job for 'The Smiler'. There was no haven for 'The Smiler'. There was no hope for 'The Smiler'. Breen's story was a sad one and a frightening one.

I had to go back to see for myself. Where Regan's had stood, there was an empty, derelict, deserted site, a mass of rubble, overgrown with charlock and nettles. I thought I could detect blackened traces on the side walls that bore out the story Breen had told me. Nobody had ever built there after the fire.

Without job, or hope, or haven, 'The Smiler' had lost none of his ingenuity. Getting in at dead of night posed no problem. He knew where the can of paraffin for the heater was kept. Five minutes would have soaked the place. A quick match to a pile of newspapers and a rapid exit as the inferno began. The fire would have got a grip immediately.

Pat and Larry were lucky to get out. By the time the alarm was raised, the old building was like a bonfire and standing across the street, in the doorway of the pub, was 'The Smiler'. He was still smiling when the Gardai took him away.

I was now standing at that very spot. Looking over at the ruins it was hard to think of the fun and the banter. It was hard to think of the songs and the stories. It was hard to think of the sunshine days.

Connie Roberts

My Irish Mother Collecting Cans In Astoria

I saw her outside Genovese one day,
her shopping cart overflowing with cans,
retrieved from putrid dumpsters, garbage bags
and picnic-waste of week-end revellers.
She stopped to light a cigarette, her old
worn out body tired, after a long
day's work. Her face aglow with pride, she pulled
her trolley closer, mumbling to herself.
She smiled a toothless-smile to all who looked
her way, that day content to be alive
and well .... and well, I couldn't help but see
my mother there in front of me....in Queens!
My God! It's her! the spit out of her mouth:
although it's July, she wears a woolen skirt
and two or three old cardigans with holes
in them pulled tightly 'round her sagging breasts
-    constant reminders of 15 kids she gave
away to nuns to rear - and nylon tights
in laced-up shoes, concealing bulbous veins
like marbles. Hair cropped short, County-Home-style,
below the ears, with clips on either side.
Arthritic fingers brown from smoke, she sucks
her cigarette as if her life depends
on it. And now she's done, she heads for home
or maybe Pathmark to sell her wares.
My heart beats fast, my breath accelerates:
"Don't go, old hag, I'm not through looking yet!"
I follow her to Steingway St., from there
to Thirty-first. She stops at Haagen Daz
and hauls her goods indoors. I follow suit.
"Good afternoon, Mary, what will it be
today .... your favourite butter-pecan?"

the Bangledesh man asks. She nods and smiles.
"Me too", I shout, "I'll have the same ...... two scoops"!
We sit at opposite tables and eat.
I watch her gum the nuts - a puppet's mouth –
chin-to-nose, chin-to-nose .... how sweet the fruits
of labour. Pale blue eyes in yellow skin
dance sprightly in her marionette-head.
She licks the spoon and smacks her lips and waves
to Mr. Khan. "Goodbye, my dear," she shouts
to me, as tears fall from my eyes. Because I
know where she's headed to: to him who lives
among the bogs of Ireland. Ogre
though he may be, she crawls right back and knocks
upon his door and lets herself be kicked
and punched, believing she deserves it all
for having strayed from husband (master): home.

Connie Roberts

Two Boys Run Away From The Orphanage
(For Ferdi)

They ran from the yard as if life depended
on it. On a whim really - not planned, thought out.
Two boys running boisterously through the town at
ten in the morning.

Out the Clara Road and on into Tubber,
they ran fast and furious, never stopping
for a moment. Running and laughing, they were
free as the wind's song.

"What will Miss Carberry say when she finds out?"
"There'll be hell to pay all round, I'm sure, but hey!
we don't care what happens, 'cause we're no longer
bound to the convent."

Soon enough their legs became tired and weary.
Stomachs grumbled noisily - sloes and berries
didn't satisfy at all. Summer rain fell
hard on their faces.

"Bet they're all enjoyin' their lunch right now, and
bet they have some strawberry tart for afters.
Bet that fella Hegarty eats my share and
yours as well. Fat pig!"

One lad came home before the other, wet and
hungry, tired and shivering. Off to bed they
sent him without sustenance, umpteen boxes
keeping his ears warm.

Several anxious faces sat up all night and

fretted for the safety of the other
boy. The clock chimed four when he walked in, frozen,
feeling so foolish
To have run away, only to return that
night. One person hugged him so tight he almost
passed out: how Miss Carberry wept to see his
freckled face light up.

Phil Robinson

Premonitions

How could she know that while asleep
The happenings in her dream were real.
She'd seen it all the night before
He'd saved her from the hurt she'd feel.
To protect her little babe within
A voice had told her she'd be strong.
Was it her guardian shielding her
Or the presence of her brother gone.
'Twas vivid in her memory
When her Dad he knocked upon her door.
He rang the bell to five then six,
She knew it had to ring once more.
Her father's footsteps in the room
Calmly she did ease her head.
She knew right then her dream was late
The brother that she loved was dead.
"What's wrong with me", says his Aunt to me
Just the day before –
Her body felt the awful weight
Before it hit our door.
Another aunt she'd seen it too
An awful tragedy,
She prayed that God would divert it
But it was not to be.
I'd walked the road two weeks before,
The coffin was raised high,
I know now God was telling me
My son was going to die.
Those signs they came from way beyond
A host of preparation,
Premonitions of what lay in store
A cruel separation.

The Three Wise Men

Michael McDonagh, Brendan Cummins and Donny Clavin

Phil Robinson

The Inquest

The coldest day we've ever had,
It made us feel so awful,
We sat there amongst a crowd
The verdict read to all out loud.
All we needed was privacy
But there indeed was not to be.
It mattered not to all the others,
Just to us parents, sisters and brothers,
The way that this young man had died.
They little cared how much we cried,
As they talked through the statement there,
His Dad sat broken in his chair,
Retracing the ordeal he had spied
On the morning that his son had died.
Why should people's tragedy
Be thrown around so publicly,
It isn't fair to open wounds
So painful out on public grounds.
Respect the ones that have to wait
Far too long after the death's date
For the verdict of the coroner,
As he spills out the awful horror
Of the happenings of some months before.
It must be held behind closed doors,
Let the powers that be hear this request -
Keep close the results of an inquest.

Eugene Sweeney

Lost Voyagers

Our ship sailed forth
On the Atlantic Sea
Against the crashing waves
And its relentless heave
We were homeless now
No strength to fight
We were driven out
By the Potato Blight
We did not know
No food was stowed
We were given room
On a floating tomb
And in that filthy hold
We shivered in fear
We lost all hope
And felt utter despair
I am shouting now
Above the roaring sea
I'm cursing the heavens
And he who might be.

Eugene Sweeney

The Banshee

By the silver stream
She scrubs and cleans
In a futile labour
Like an endless dream
For that blood-soaked shroud
She can never clean
An omen of death
Is what it means
She is a siren
An angel of death
This is her announcement
A soul to collect
For those who hear
Her haunting cries
Her sobbing and wailing
And her endless sighs
Look towards the heavens
And not her eyes
For those who do
Its their own demise

Eugene Sweeney

Our Planet

I have read in books
About times gone by
Of lush green grass
And the animal life
We had so much
And life was good
But now our greed
Has cleared our woods
The forests are few
The animals have gone
Can we be proud
Of what we have done
What we have left
We must not neglect
For our future generation
We must all protect
This planet so fair
For which we little care
We must restock so all can share
Its beauty, its life, its atmosphere.

Teresa Kelly

Pause

Lightly
throw me a rope
don't panic me
like a dog
might
worry a sheep
throwing him back
into a corner.

Lightly
throw me a rope
look the other way
while I
circle the ground
create a sound
stoop
to lift the cord
brush the twisted flax.

When the moment comes
to move,
can you be there
to pull in the slack?

Teresa Kelly

South of Paris

Wooden gates to sunflower
fields, two bicycles
rollmop dips and bends
through highlit summer.
At a fish farm
we catch our evening meal

My job to gut the fish
methods gleaned from
cordon bleu,
you worked in a fish factory
different schools.

Seismic anger, we retreat
to opposite ends of the
room. In silence
the fish become silken
debris, their fate assured.
Much later
our bodies kiss,
the abyss lingers.

Joe Finlay relaxing in Annie Kelly's

Teresa Kelly

Imprint

Touch soft touch
irredeemable quality
I had reason not to trust

in your quarry.
You arrived
a thumb on a motorway

it leaves a mark,
a sleeping arm
across my belly.

I wondered for an age
at the difference
between men and women

a safe place to wander
with light overhead;
calm seas and charted water.

Still it changes
in your features,
my fear, a bolt undone

leashing into life
strange winds
to harvest the storm.

Teresa Kelly

For Jim

How does it feel
watching the goings on
from another dimension,

have you met anyone
we know and greeted
them with the same lack
of preamble as before.

The news came this evening
sudden and brutal
no incarceration
in a hospital bed.

The childhood delight
of your visits,
the great unknown
within the sphere
of our kitchen floor
six foot and more.

In Glasgow, a student
clad in second hand skin
unformed ideas
grist to your mill
survival stolid company.

Can you understand
the need to paper over,
the fear that niceties
should become undone
too quick.

I begin to glimpse,
what clean cut lines
reveal, the adult child
of our dreams
rarely rests in peace.

Maureen Lowndes

The Field

You can hear her wail in the wind
as she pulls the stalk of putrid squash
from the soft yielding earth.
Distraught from the black hunger, she falls,
with the child suckling at her barren breast.
She pleads in vain to the heavens as the
claws of death envelop her and the fruit
of her womb.

Listen. You can hear the cry of the young
man. See the black terror in his blue eyes
as he runs through the field.
He stumbles and falls amidst a hail of gun
fire, fired by Black and Tan soldiers.
The marauding invaders smile and cheer at
the echo of his dying cry, and the
field red with his fresh young blood.

As the wheels of progress travelled through
time the hedgerows planted with care by the hands of
our forefathers were flattened by gigantic
bellowing machines and incinerated to ashes and
dust. Mingled with cold black earth, just
like those who proudly planted with their raw,
callused and bare hands long ago before you
and I were born.

As the silage harvester gobbles and chops the
last row of thick green forage, the field
is bare, barren, bleak and cold like the
hearts of our ancestors.

Maureen Lowndes

Reflections of An Old Man

Seated on the hard wooden desk.
Sore arse, rigid back and bare feet.
Blasted teacher bashed my head with a
nobbledy pole.
For the horrendous crime of daring
Look back at Mary Jane.
Terrible crime.

Sixpence a day for pulling beet and
pulling turnips.
For the obese hairless farmer.
I did manage to get the big tall daughter
to lie down at the back of the hay reek.
Fuck that.

Old and dotty now.
Children emigrated to Athens and
Termonfeckin.
And they wearing wool suits and satin
knickers.
And they cohabiting in four poster
beds with lace drapes.
Double fuck that.

My frail weak body soon to be snuffed out
like a wasted Christmas candle.
Face crinkled like a well used barley
sack will grimace and cringe with pain.
Moan, drown in a sea of perspiration.
Treble fuck that.

Maureen Lowndes

Prisoner in Mountjoy

Door slammed.
Key driven angrily home.
Your mind beating,
like the waves of some far off ocean.
They can't think like you think.
They can't feel like you feel.
No one to heal the pain.
They don't care.

Dogs are barking,
in a sprawling estate,
somewhere out there in the city.
A drab worn out woman.
A battered blossom.
Lost in a world of shattered dreams.
No empathy for her prisoner son.
They don't care.

In your cell.
Sleep interrupted by dreams.
A five year old battered in a drunken rage.
Sound of wicked voices hurling up the stairs.
Ghosts from the past torment your quiescent hours.
Someone screams, it is you.
No one to nurture the inner child in you.
They don't care.

Maureen Lowndes

Nephew's New Girl

She is a teacher you know,
and she has a brother
a solicitor in Mallow.

Said old Aunt Nell,
speaking of her nephew's
new girl.

She is a fine match,
what a great catch.
Bragged old Aunt Nell,
while she lay buried in
the bed beside old
Uncle Ted.

Old Aunt Nell is a snob.
She married Uncle Ted
back in the time of
the rations,
and Hitler trying to take
the world.

Aunt Nell might be misled.
The teacher might be a whore.
The solicitor might be a crook.
And he might be better with a
factory girl.

Derek Fanning

'May my Heart'

May my heart be forever gentle
And never a masculine, unfeeling thing;
May my soul be forever present
And never submerged, forlorn.
This world of capitalism continuously threatens
To rot our hearts, to destroy our souls.
We grow old, we grow old,
Our time is short upon this world;
Let us live, let us live
And not forego our Greatest Gift,
Our Gift of Insight.

When I shine I shine with a furious force -
It is born of Insight –
It will not die, it must out –
This passionate power, this incredible
          phenomenon
Is indomitable, everlasting.
It is a thing of extraordinary beauty,
          incredible wisdom,
And it will not let me rest,
It must have dominance;
And it rebels against capitalism
Making me a rebel against capitalism;
This force, this unquenchable force.

May my heart be forever gentle
And never a masculine, unfeeling thing.
May this world of Non-Insight
Never rot my heart and soul.

Conferring at the Bar

Jimmy Dromey, Brendan Cummins and Donny Clavin.

These are my thoughts as I walk down
      Adylsu Valley
In the Causcasus Mountains;
These are my thoughts as I leave
      behind the world
And wander into this Place of Insight.

Derek Fanning

'Deluded Souls'

Deluded souls trample like bovine brutes
through the sickening spectacle of existence;
They belch like gluttonous pigs fattened
on the filthy produce of the world;
Their fingers are grasping, slimy, reeking
of the nauseating excrescences they create;
Their minds made narrow by stinking logic
(Logic - the death of the soul!) –

When will it end?
When will it end O Lord my God?

And yet I am one of these too –
Do not forget it.

We are the Spectres of the Earth,
More brutes than men,
Lashed to our status quo, unquestioning,
like mindless lemmings,
Besotted with our narrowness,
Besotted with our futility.

When will it end?
When will it end O Lord my God?
ECCE HOMO & WEEP!

This is the way matters transpired –
On acquiring logic we shed our babe-like
    innocence
& descended into the Abyssal Monstrosity
        of what it is to be human;

Since then hardly anyone has had the pluck,
        the courage,
        to be different,
        truly different,
        apart from the herd.
Our Mind-Prison has fabricated a bizarre,
        nightmarish Game,
The Game of Life,
The Game of day to day living.

How to get on?
Simple - conform. Play the Game.

When will it end?
When will it end O Lord my God?
ECCE HOMO & WEEP!
And yet I am one of these too –
Do not forget it.
I too have been hurled unwittingly
        into the Game
& I am compelled to play

Fuck the lot of them!
Fuck the bastards & their fucking Game!

Tom Murray

The Twelve Pins

Ever shy and reticent
With features shrouded
In the shimmering veils
Of an ever changing Connemara mist
Now white, now grey, now blue.

Seldom undressing until
The warmth of some noonday sun
Exerts its gentle persuasion,
Then casting their modesty
To the west wind
They gently bare the wild and lusty beauty
Of curved breast and classic shoulder
Moulded a million years ago.

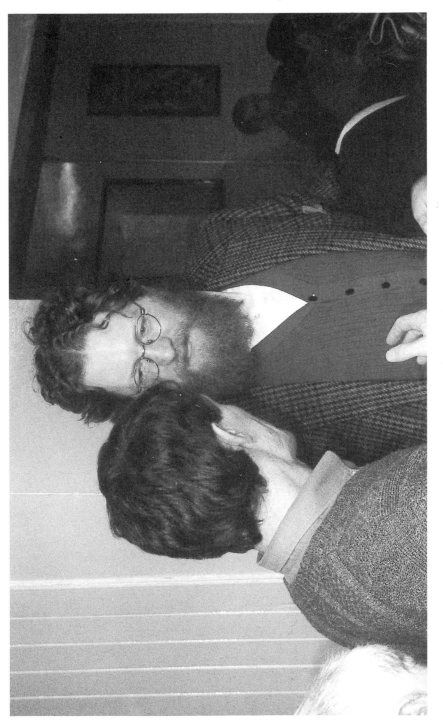

Derek Fanning mixing metaphors with Brendan Cummins.

Michael Donegan

Poem From The Front

Father I cannot sleep.
Like paralysed pools
Abandoned among
Wire
You lie forever
Outside my grasp.
If only I could hold your
Head, gently,
Rocking you in the bowl
Of elbow and chest.

I have been so
Long standing here
My feet rot
And the roars
Of the dying
Are terrible
Through nose and
Ears they pierce
My head.

But I am still on fire
In my searching
from mound to mound
a twitching rat.
I run
To pick you out
From all the
Other dead.

Michael Donegan

Mary Ann

At 78 Mary Ann Flannery burns rubbish with a relish
Makes hell in a tar barrel
Of bail twine and bags
And polystyrene packing
And even defies combustion with potato skins.

Windlike her whistle of words
Calls up the dead
To bless the newly birthed lambs
Old ewe-midwife burden beast.

When hay straggles the ditches
And bullocks hump the wind
She tacks armada-like to fend for hens
Or apron-barrow turf across the scattered yard.

Empress of cans, the hollow
Lowing of calves pipe her
The wisdom of things unwritten.
Distant as the distant shouts of men to horses,
Through all the dull rattle of the years,
The days when fields were lost to rain
Or when wells dried and the haggards bulged with corn.

She is,
A stone tossed sideways
By the struggle of an ancient load.
The crow man breast-high in the corn.
A gate half-closed into an evening field.
The sound of laughter on a leafy road.

Michael Donegan

Phone Call

Tonight the digits chittered
My need of you
To you
And belled
Frantically
Through your
House
to no one,
Belted off walls
And panicked
Among furniture,
Even searched
Your pillow
And all the quiet spaces
That you fill
Remained
Impassive,
Faithfully
Awaiting
Your homecoming.

Mary Dunne

My Father

He was not a God.
He never was nor could he ever be,
yet he behaved like one and in those moments
I believed that he was.
I blame myself for this
because in my mind I wanted him to be greater
than any other man.
I created the perfect idol,
lived my youth in the shadow
of an all-knowing, all-seeing Tower of Wisdom.
The awe of his majesty scared me.
It was unbelievable that one brain could hold
so much knowledge. The mysteries of the Universe,
the flood gates of his mind,
the riddle of Simplicity,
and the pure Intelligence that was his to command.
And thus he accepted the adulation of a child,
and thus he outgrew the mortal skin of man
and began to believe in my Fantasia.
I had manifested the icon of perfection
and saw little beyond the mystique of my own intellect.
My feet remained in the earth,
never losing touch with my own reality,
but I lost the true image of him somewhere.
In the translation from youth to maturity
a developing mind overtook the fear of awe,
and in the culture shock that followed,
his crown slipped and the king lost favour.
The bitter realisation brought shame
and misplaced anger directed itself
entirely against the God and not the creator.
He was not omniscient.

Séan O'Connor and Sheila Daly listening to the yarns of Donny Clavin.

He was human
and I couldn't accept that.
He is my father and king in my eyes forever
The king died on the 7th Dec 1995.
And the child in me still cries out.

Mary Dunne

The Mouse

From a little hole in the corner
he comes sniffing, twitching, scratching.
Tiny feet pitter-pattering,
sliding, slipping on smooth-polished surfaces.
Brown furry coat shimmering in the shadows,
dark eyes shifting, studying, piercing the night.
Little ears listening, tuned in, twittering.
At first darting, now pausing,
scurrying, skulking, sneaking,
prying, hiding biding his time.
Whiskers piercing the night
like feathers brushing the wind.
Long tail, ever swishing, ever following
from shade to shade across the vast, empty
expanses of plush carpet.
Sensitive nose quivering, exploring the air.
Smell of polish, smell of wood,
smell of food, *cheese!*
Gold - mountains of it!
A blinding, yellow beauty ...
Gotya!
Snap!
Squelch!

Gone!

Vera Hughes

Black Dog

Days are the worst-
long hours to kill,
watching the clock,
seeing people go by
in the street,
hearing footsteps that never
stop at my door.
Waiting for the darkness
and sleep,
dreading the night-
dreading the approach
of yet another night.

Nights are the worst-
when sleep won't come,
and the mind can't rest,
counting the hours,
getting up to make tea,
listen to the radio,
talk to the cat.
Hearing night sounds
in the street,
waiting for daylight,
and dreading the dawn-
dreading the dawn
of yet another day.

Vera Hughes

Annunciation

In the day's tumult and clamour,
a moment of quiet –
the Angelus bell rings.
Again.

A rustle of wings.

Gabriel's awesome news

proclaimed to Mary.

The maid compliant.

The Word made Flesh.

The world redeemed.

The measured tolling ends.
The day's tumult and clamour.
Again.

Sobering Thoughts

Bríd Broderick, Mary Margaret Guinan, Teresa Kelly

Dr. Alec Hughes (1924-1998)

Leaba Sioda   "Bed of Silk"

I lie, Ballybunion baths,
wreathed in sea-wrack,
luxuriating
in the silkiness
of the iodine weed,
a laurel around my head,
my feet wrapped in weed,
the hot water steaming,
the aesthetic pleasure of
soaking in my sea-weed bed.

I am a Roman Emperor,
happy hedonist,
after a cerebrating, celebrating week
of Poetry Workshop in Listowel.
The Muse rules my seat of pleasure,
and I am free.
There is a harmony
of sea and weed.

My inward spirit flows
with peace,
harmony exudes through my pores.
The nimbus of my silken glow
will stay for ever.

Dr. Alec Hughes (1924-1998)

Patsy

Patsy, rogue and schemer,
with the gilt of healing in his tongue,
spinner of yarns and traditional tales;
he could recall his father,
born before the Famine,
evicted from his hovel,
and forced for years to wander,
till he settled in this bogland home.

At the age of seventy, on St. John's Eve,
he swallowed live an "allapluca"
a yellow-bellied lizard — after three decades
of his beads, — and so got his healing tongue.
The cure was in his spittle –
burns, and all skin afflictions,
he could lick clean away,
within the space of fifteen days.
White-haired like a prophet,
in his little lime-washed cottage,
the donkey cart waited outside,
in case of urgent need.

Mrs. Kyne, his neighbour,
elderly and stooped-shouldered,
one freezing Winter night,
went out to do her chores
watched the heifer calving,
and when she heard the lowing
of the new-born calf,
came in numb with cold,
and quickly put her bum
against the glowing Stanley range.

When her husband smelled
the smouldering clothes,
and heard the woman's roars,
he poured a pail of water
on her, prostrate on the floor,
then went for the man who had the cure.

In his donkey cart, Patsy came,
with leisurely haste,
and licked the affected part,
to relieve the pain,
so after fifteen successive nights
of judicious oral healing,
Mrs. Kyne was made whole again.

Brid Broderick

Night-light

I hear you calling me
in city streets
in country lanes
in attic rooms

I feel you calming me
thro' sleepless nights
while working late
when sleeping late

I feel you speak to me
from endless poems
from endless songs
from endless words

I feel you comfort me
with words
with wishes
with wisdom

I see you in the sunshine
I sleep with you in dreams

Between the Reels and the Rhymes

Liam Daly and Jim Brennan.

Brid Broderick

Carrig Mór

waking to the smell of fresh coffee
waking to the smell of squeezed oranges
waking to the smell of turf fire
waking to the smell of love

walking up Kileenacoff hill
walking through bracken
walking through heather
walking through gorse

tracing long-ago life-lines
standing stone to circle to tomb
all paths leading to
the hill of silence

Carol Burke

The New Me

Like a rocket to the moon
Life exploded all around me!
Thoughts welled up in my head
To overflow - unheeded and
Unchecked.
This was a new experience –
My feelings went into overdrive,
They pitched and fell and heaved –
Leaving me dizzy.
I was hitting life in spots –
Knocking off the rough edges.
And while doing so - I neatly
Pleated in white tissue paper
A part of me - so real and
So familiar to the touch –
No! Not a part but all of me
The old me!

Maureen Comerford

Memories Of Mayo - 1950's

I was born in the townsland of Doiremhór near Westport Co Mayo - the first of a large family. Our home was surrounded by mountains whose proud tops touched the clear sky. Sometimes they disappeared into the mist for days on end to re-emerge all shiny and washed with silver rivers hanging from their summits. These rivers appeared only after rain and rain was our constant companion in that beautiful valley.

The mountains had old Irish names: Lug an Óir, Cnoc Mór, Gleann Lára, Láchta and standing proud and majestic to the north was "The Reek". My father, a lean, hardy man knew every inch of these mountains. In fine weather I often accompanied him on sheep gathering trips to the foothills. I can still see us trekking that rough terrain my three steps to his one. As we walked he would tell me about the mountains, explaining their names, pointing out the famine ridges and he would stop to show me old ruins which were once homes to families who are now in far off New York, Boston or Philadelphia. The vastness of the valley was breathtaking, the silence broken only by sheep bleating in the distance or the sound of a nearby river. The rivers had different moods, sometimes they were placid and lazily meandered along. Other times they were raging torrents, their dark waters full of suds angrily rushing to the sea, so angry were they at times that they burst their banks and swept away crops and sheep. My father would then complain about the 'anró [1]' of trying to survive in these parts.

In wintertime the milking was done after dark. I held the lantern as my father's strong hands milked the cows. The cow house was cosy with golden straw for bedding. As the cows contentedly chewed their cuds the wind rose occasionally and got through the old door causing my lantern to flicker. How secure I felt there seeing the cat appear from the rafters for her supper of warm creamy milk. When the bucket was full we went inside the thatched cottage. My mother welcomed the new milk which she strained immediately. She pitied us for being out on such awful nights. The kitchen was aglow with the oil lamp lighting and the big open fire throwing out heat as far as the door. Grandmother was tucked away in the 'cailleach[2]' from where she kept an eagle eye on the goings on. The door was closed and we enjoyed hot cocoa at the fire.

At eight o'clock the Rosary beads were taken down and we all got on our knees. My father gave out the rosary, the older children said a decade each while mother recited the Litany of The Blessed Virgin Mary: "Tower of Ivory", "House of God", "Ark of the Covenant", "Morning Star". We responded to each strange title with "Pray for us". My parents thanked God for the day that was ending and we resumed our positions around the fire. Soon the latch was lifted and in stepped our neighbour with the greeting "God save all here". He was welcomed warmly and given the best seat near the fire. This visitor brought all the latest news from the neighbourhood and if he was in town lately he would also bring a newspaper. All major world events such as Cuba, Cyprus, Suez were discussed at length and the great pride that was felt when Grace Kelly married her prince. As well as these serious conversations there was plenty of fun and laughter. Storytelling was a real treat with special emphasis on ghost stories. Occasionally other visitors came bringing musical instruments - music and song would follow. My special memory is of Peggy McLoughlin's rendition of "The Moon Behind the Hill" sparked off by the view from our tiny kitchen window of a full golden moon rising in a clear, frosty sky from behind Lug an Óir. Grandmother contributed from the "cailleach", but when she felt it was time to call a halt she hopped out of bed and started to wind the clock.

She was a small sprightly woman with long white hair which she wore in a bun held with hairpins. Seven of her eleven children were in America and on fine days she would sit on a rock halfway down the boreen, waiting for the postman, hoping for news from them. As I sat with her she told me about coming to the valley as a young bride. She came from Aughagower - ten miles away and she was only eighteen yeas old. Her husband was almost twice her age and she had met him only once before the wedding. As she travelled to the chapel on horseback, she recalled being of two minds as to whether to go ahead or turn back. She decided to go ahead, a decision she never regretted for he was a quiet kind man whom she grew to love.

Unfortunately, love alone could not feed a large family. My grandfather, who was a gaelic speaker was forced to leave his pregnant wife, ten children, this scenic valley and head for Chicago. Here he joined his brother and worked on the railroads for many years before returning, by which time some of the older children had left for America. This meant that the entire family were never all together. The youngest child was almost an adult by the time she first met her father. Soon after his return my grandparents had the heartbreak of seeing six more of their children depart for Boston - four on the same day. Grandfather died at an advanced age in 1938, my grandmother lived to the ripe old age of ninety four and had the joy of seeing all but one of her family return to visit her on several occasions. Today their descendents from all over the USA come to see that old thatched cottage which is now almost derelict. But the valley is as beautiful as ever and to me it was paradise then and somehow it still is.

[1] 'anró' - A word used locally meaning hardship.
[2] 'cailleach' - A bed built into the wall in the kitchen usually near the fire.

Fiona McKeown

A Boy I Once Knew

I once knew a boy
He was as good as gold
You'd never see him bold
But as he grew up
He got in with the wrong crowd
Every night you'd hear them
And boy were they loud
Then he started with the drugs
Because of them he looked like a terrible thug
Soon police came knocking on his door
They searched his house
Found drugs everywhere even under the floor
He then started in crime
His parents, for them it really was a bad time
Everyone thought he was a nice boy
Whatever happened to him and his now forgotten toys.

Giving a Tip at Annie Kelly's .
Séan O'Connor and Finnian Robbins

Ann Egan

The Sewing Girl To Her Mother
(In Memory of Mrs. Eileen O'Connor)

Cross stitch on even weave,
back stitch on block weave.

I am the sewing girl, sit on a hard chair
head bent to my task. Repair elbow and knee
tauten selvedge northwards, mould my weft
to crescent shapes of lively joints that leap

and loop in childish play or hoop with long
labour in fields of waving hay, crackling oats.
Buntings flutter on thorny bushes, I patch
their void with flower thread, weave motifs

of daisychain days, capture the call
of young voices in seesaw forests.
With a skein of blue I braid the sky
buttercup perle of cotton frame droplets

of sun, stay and sew my adventures,
mitre corners, guided by seagreen eyes
I pipe my seam to your words.
I am your sewing girl.

Cross stitch on even weave,
back stitch on block weave.

Ann Egan

The Seaman
(For Tim O'Connor)

Bound and fettered
to the family farm,
season in, season out,
he follows forebears,

sea gnaw whittles
away innards
as trickle water
wears stone.

When spring lures,
he yokes up Kit and Sal,
holds the ploughhandle
with a sailor's grip,

ship's wheel
in a ruffled sea,
winds hiss,
gulls grey-white

flash, cavort, dive.
Tramples headland
to black headland,
trenches firm sod,

cast up root
intertwined,
as amber seaweed
halved red worms

wriggle in confusion.
Earth ripples,

folds and falls,
steadies sideways,
hip hop
insects flee
bronze sparks free
from plaited clay.

'Hup now, hup,'
he sighs harnessed,
for crimped earth is
ever solid.

Ride green waves,
curry opal foam,
sea-horses buck
and leap over water,

chasms gape,
hungry for sailors.
Swingletrees sway
port to larboard,

nib and sock burrow,
counter follows wing,
board turns
the scrape over,

and he plods on,
ploughing the furrows
of his sea dream.

Ann Egan

A Nun's Last Corncrake
(for Sr. Raphael Egan)

Her sky dips on a sloped field,
fingers a ditch's nook where
the Glenbarrow's a pool of lights,

tail swishes of brown and gold,
threatening silver as a bog
languishes in scents of heather.

Her river-in-waiting gathers
swelling runnels to its core
while stones gouged by shard and scree,

clay cradles for pioneering flowers.
Reed whispers from a will-o'-the wisp banks
arc her convent from the city's babble,

while one corncrake pierces the dam
of solitary words walled in her mind,
floods her soul with listening talk.

Sean O'Connor

Sisyphean

Perusing beneath her portrait, I found
Her epitaph, deep in the lexicon.
And recalling my image of stone, bound
Downhill, I saw her labour in the sun
And weary tho' she was, she turned and smiled
A maternal smile, accepting this test
Of raw love imposed by a callous child,
That tied her to this task to know no rest.

And tho' guilt of yesteryear has haunted
This heart that once was hard, her endurance
Was my saviour, while her love, undaunted,
Paved a peaceful path for my assurance.
Somewhere stands a stone covered with soft moss.
Nearby, she's now resting, free from her cross.

(Cissy Feehan 1916-1988)

Sean O'Connor

Outcasts

Our skin is just as fair, but in your sight
It's as black as the winding Irish lanes
Stretching out into the bleak winters night.
We belong to her ditches and her drains,
Where the canvas-muffled cry of lesser
Children, disperses like smoke from the fire.
We were the first-born of the Oppressor,
Must we still wear the mantle of the briar?

My heart is just as true, but in your mind
It's full of wanderlust, longing for green
Valleys. A restless soul, hitched to the wind,
You curtain off the hardships we have seen.
Tho' weary of the road and traffic's din
Still, we search in vain for the 'The Welcome Inn'.

Sean O'Connor

Island Girl

Her fantasies and dreams
Were like a myriad of tiny boats,
Babbling in the harbour
Loosely tethered, standing by
To take her to far flung exotic places,
Away from the harsh realities of island life.

Unnoticed, one by one they slipped
Their mooring, and drifted out to sea.
Catching sight of her last dreamboat
As it dipped below the blue horizon,
She heard only the silence of the rocks
As they cast long shadows on her last sunset.

Paul Egan

The Past

A lonely desolate,
Steaming wreck of a place
With strewn hearts and souls
And burst minds
And wandering foreign fools.

An emotional rubbish tip
Of poisonous spewing incidents
Of buried memories and smoldering emotions,
Left festering under the glare of the sun
and the cutting wind.

Where have you buried me?
I said to the silver pain.
What have you done with the map of perfection?
Why it's in yourself of course, you fool
Where I knew you would never look,
amongst stinking flesh and splinted bone.

Georgina Brennan Nee Conroy

Dockside Blues

Secured with a leather belt,
A small brown, battered, suitcase,
Clutched tightly by his side.
He stands alone, surrounded by
Hundreds more, as he waits
Wearly by the dock side.

Another trip across the sea.
His black heavy overcoat, the
Only barrier against the rough
cold weather, building sites
Draughty railway stations,
Salvation Army overnight, or
FLEA ridden cheap hotel accommodation.

His heart is heavy like the night
With thought of home embraced
By his loving wife.
Curse the devil upon this rough
Sea crossing, his prayers to God
Had ceased, no job, no security,
Upon his own shore.

His fifty bob won't last forever.
Sixth sense already touched the
Hunger pangs felt before, his packet
Of Afton cigarettes, once shared,
Guaranteed a lasting friendship,
On a foreign English shore.

Another lonely soul dressed in
A donkey jacket, extends a chapped
Weathered hand, and lighted match.
His story is perhaps the same or

Further down the line, a man dressed
In a donkey jacket, to do a donkeys
Work, hired as a labourer on a
Building site, or to lift and haul
Heavy sleepers upon a railway line.

No dole queues, or welfare bank giros,
For these men of 1965, only heartache
Lonely hours working in cement and muck.
Empty nights, empty stomachs, young men
WITH haggard faces that was reality back then.

Geraldine Brosnahan

Widening Doors

The leather coat,
black, cold and unyielding,
like you
in the wrong mood,
gradually
softens and warms,
crushed in my arms.

A seventies relic,
more my time
than yours,
of cheap papery hide,
bought for twelve pounds fifty,
from a damp,
depressing Oxfam shop.

I picture the coat,
confident with fresh life,
swinging its way
through strange new doors
widening fast,
to accommodate your hopes
and aspirations.

When it wraps around you,
in places far from here,
I'll will your thoughts,
to arms that cradled
and nursed,
and gave you to the world
with grace.

Geraldine Brosnahan

Monday

Monday daylight mist,
has the nailmarks of night,
still clinging to its gown,
as she rises from the bed,
first up in the street.

The tap gushes,
drumming the kettle bottom,
then a satisfying hiss
as flame and wet copper collide,
bringing life in a lifeless house.

Toast and rusty tea,
perched on a tray of wood,
that mourns faded flowers,
that once adorned it,
and assorted hands that held.

Once, time was short,
and childish giggles
and manly laughter filled a house
where cakes were baked.
And potatoes peeled.
And life was lived.

Black plastic bag waits,
focus of this particular day,
carefully bow-tied last night,
during the break in
Coronation Street.

Sipping and swallowing,
by fire with plastic coals,
one eye on breakfast t.v.
ear tuned for the rumble
of the bin lorry.

Michael Egan

Why?

With money being the root of all evil
We will then never find peace when we
Totally depend on money to survive.
Our twenty-first century is approaching fast
Our status quo has failed.
Why not make it a part of our history?
Why not work to make it happen?
Why not learn how to kill the thirst?
Why not peacefully celebrate the twenty-first?
Why support destruction and pain?
Why not learn how to use your brain?
Why not ask the intensely kind?
Why continue to be blind?
Why not learn how to live in peace?
Why it's there if you please.
Why not stop and take a look?
Why not explore a wisdom book?
Why not learn how to evolve?
Why lack knowledge and let life dissolve?
Why, tell me why?
Why let our world die?
Why let there be a cry?
Why make strange?
Why not change?

Eileen Casey

Beyond The Blue Door

The name above the shop
then an incline onto bare wood,
my step a stumble of impatience.

Eyes adjust to jumbles of dishcloths,
hurly sheaves.
Dolls with squeaky bellies wear necklaces
of rosaries, beads brown as aniseed.
Loose playing cards. Always
the Jack of Hearts.

Breakfast mug in hand,
the Huckster makes an entrance
from an opening in an alcove.
Behind that blue door
he lives the life
my imagination has made flesh.
Where a radio crackles,
clocks are wound and placed on cluttered shelves,
an unmade bed, photographs.

Though its colour's paler now
that blue door, the Huckster
moving beyond it,
takes me past the dusty incline
down to echoing boards.

Eileen Casey

Peat

Water soldier, bulrush, gipsywort,
birch.
Turfbrown shades,
firesmoke, firesmell.

Star moss, feather moss,
cowberry, crowberry,
bogblood.
Constant as rainpulses
over Pollagh, over Clara
where rannock rushes grow.

Yellowflower bogbursts
flecking flat landscapes
of bogpeople.

I am of the bogpeople,
of firesmoke, firesmell.

In textured layers,
pine, bogrosemary, burgundy red bogmoss,
water horsetail, diandrous sedge,
preservation.

Eileen Casey

Clockwise

A man once told me, time was all
he learned at school.

How sharp those morning angles
must have read, as the clockface
split in two. Latecomers thrashed,
homework sweated over,
given up.

At mid-day, time folding in
hung a moonshape above
blackboards clouds, where numbers
chalked infinity.
So it went,

afternoons quartered into tense
into fraction. Until a tiny fan
at five past three, measured out
the agony, and heartbeats
raced with seconds
to embrace the final hour.

Poetry Lovers

Geraldine Brosnahan and Phil Newton.

Eileen Casey

The Love of my Sixteenth Year

A convent girl,
I walked the long way home
as you did from the Brothers
to prowl the town for sightings.

From opposite sides of Mainstreet
we gauged a parallel,
watched corner mirrors
in jewelers
for angles of approach.
When it rained
we huddled into doorways
or sheltered under canopies
or stared into drapery windows
red-faced by displays
of women's things.
Two decades later,

we pass each other
close enough to touch
at the precise moment
on the moving stairway
of a shopping centre.
our eyes transfix

Jim Brennan

Over the High Bank

Way out in the early wood
Before the birds awake
All sleeping things are startled
To hear the corncrake.

Here in the stillness of the fog
Her cry calls out a warning sound
In Ballylennon where men
With their slans and forks

Walk along a short soft road
To cut the year's first turf
Out of the wet ground where
The bog oak sleeps.

The sweet smell is everywhere
From the high bog
The heather is cut and rolled down
Into last years black water.

There hidden underneath
The dark rich layers
Are opened up to feel
The morning heat of April sun.

But will she be heard
Calling across time
Over the high bank
Her voice still warning
When all is quiet
In Ballylennon bog.

Jim Brennan

The Straws Edge

The soft line of thatch
Was easy on the eye then
Where the sun caught
The straws edge.
The gable rolled down
In its own time.

When windows had no definite line
Each one its own size
Looking out from
Stout broad walls
At crab apple trees

My mother and her brother Jim
Their mother
And her mother
Sitting down beside him,
Look at me from sixty years ago
Resting there from their morning's work
Milking early
Then making butter

Scooping flour out of white soft sacks
And spooning dry tea from deep inside
A silver line chest
That came all the way from India

Going up to Coffeys shop
And racing home with striped red sweets
Secrets there inside brown paper bags
When the soft line was easy on the eye
And the sun caught the straws edge.

Jim Brennan

Measuring

Some of them I met
When I was young
That generation who would
Cut and plane and measure out
With little folding timber rulers
Inches feet and yards
All down through the days
Of my father's time.

I watched him once
When I was five years old
Making windows for Danny Hanlon's house
The sound of sawing in the shed
The plane swishing down across
Made curls of wood
Fall down around his feet.

I picked them up in my small hands
And can still smell the sweet pine scent
My father smiled down at me
And made a wig of curly wood
Hang down around my ears.

Sometimes still I see him
Marking timber in the shed
Counting out his years and days
Until shadows from a candle
Flicker quiet across his face

Deep to me his grave was dug
Down into the August clay
Men cut the green grass

Straight with spades
They measured out the length and breadth

Tight in my hand I held
That folding timber ruler
Then let it fall
Down into nowhere
To the clay
Beneath his head.

E.L. Biffo

On The Road

The old Morris Minor rolled
slowly round the monastery bend
stuttered
as it started up the hill
the driver offering encouragement
"giddy up there Bessie"
I was at the back seated forward
pestering
when it happened
She snapped
an exasperated reply
I stopped, stunned
and fell back in a heap.
My mother had told a lie.

E.L. Biffo

Flaggin'

The smell of frying rashers wafting
to the spit and sizzle of Tullamore sausages
as the rain cools my aching head.
From my outstretched thumb tiny
rivulets of rainwater trickle
down benignly beneath my sleeve.
"Crucify him" I scream as a
priest swooshes by in his
big, empty, spacious, 'company' car.
Children struggle past under enormous schoolbags
as a fat man dashes out to take the milk
and flaunt his rear-end cleavage.
I dream of roast beef, dried feet, steaming mugs of
homemade soup and creamy pints of porter
escape from wringing reality, profanity, insanity.
"Hitchin?....................on yer fuckin' bike"

Jackie Gorman

A Room With Sunlight

After the audience with the Dalai Lama, I took a taxi back to my hotel in Boudanath. In this VW Golf, back to my room, I gave my good wishes to the world in front of me and behind me.

I opened the windows and let the sunlight and wind come in.
I lay face down on the bed. Over my right shoulder, I could see the sunset in the gardens. I could feel the hot Asian breeze at the base of my spine. Once when you put your hands there, I dived into an ocean with a yellow setting sun. The evening passed on with a full moon. I was aware of incoming tides been dragged backwards, of my own silence, no longer where I thought I was.

Jackie Gorman

Running Faster

I found a photo of my father in his vest, standing by the turf shed. A hot Summer's day and Granny is saying something to my mother. The hedge long since cut down looks lovely and a Holly Hobby sits forever on the wheelbarrow.

I remember the May Altar on our front doorstep the pungent smell of freshly picked gorse intoxicating the hallways of our house. A tradition that has long since been bypassed to another time.

I imagine him surrounded by family and friends - taking refuge with them. Jackie Roper, Bunny Roper, Eddie Harrigan, Frank Kenny. 'Hardy' gentlemen who have stepped from the edges of my childhood to another place.

Dinner is finished and he is hatching in the chair by the range. His head is turned to make a smart remark and he has folded his hands around 'the Irish Press'. The kettle boils slowly.

The voice that called over soggy Coosan fields to hurry me home. I am running faster. I want to tell that I am at the back of Hanevy's house and I'm nearly there. Seeing the light in the back kitchen and hearing the watery sound of a filling kettle, seeing the light at the end of the world and I am running faster.

Jackie Gorman

Larks in Silence

From the walk of raised stones, we reach the mossy hillside. It softens to our step, our touch. A skylark begins its ascent to the upper townlands of the skies.

We reach a final slab, a final thought and from here we can see the entire landscape. You tell me that down below battles were fought and up here the warriors were healed with water and herbs.

We lie down to be healed. Senses cleansed, the larks grow in number. They begin a frenzy of cries, a challenge to the silence. A curious landscape gathers around us in wonder.

Carol Kavanagh

Freedom

The first step felt so good,
My heart fluttered.
As a bird would take off,
Releasing its wings releasing me.

The first sight of beauty,
The sun and the sky,
Heat passed on my face,
Just its presence was comforting.

Never again would I return,
Hide me away from that retched mind.
Keep me safe in this paradise, away from pain,
Keep that beast far from my bruised body.

That beast insane.

Ber Brophy

The Passing

Dim lit room and muffled tones
Tears of bitter grief.
One last goodbye, a final kiss
Mortality. The passing.

Flowers bright and music soft
Eerie chiming bells.
Time will fade the inner pain
But memories stay. The passing.

Dust thou art and into dust
A grave reality.
To meet up in a different world
Another day. The passing.

23 Larkfield Avenue

How are they all in Birr?
Is the Mundy lad still
At the music,
And did the Dom get his fill
From Enright's
On Tuesday night?
Has Allie said hi
To the folks in Larkfield
Since we sealed our departure?
Is Ronan's ulcer still
Belching in the morning?
Is Niall still breaking
Bedroom windows and waking
You up with the guitar?
And Joe, is he still mean
With the coke and keen
For Ronan to iron shirts?
Is Rory's van still blocking
Up the driveway
And ruining the bikes
That can't get past it?
Has Emma still her nose
Pierced, and Sinead, I suppose
She's still at the massage?
Is the house still like
The Bermuda Triangle,
With the telly on
At the back wall?
Or is there anyone
There at all?

Ann Tyrell-McCormack

Knots

Lying down,
Tied in knots,
Eyes moving
Only to see
Who wants me now,
What for!

Sampling the Atmosphere at Annie Kelly's.
Freda Rowntree, Olivia O'Toole and Tom Scully.

Denis Wrafter (1910-1996)

Offaly's Hurling Stock

Where ash trees rise from limestone earth,
That fertile spine from Tullamore,
Between Slieve Bloom and Shannon's girth,
Killoughey and Drumcullen roared.
The old Abul of O'Molloy.

And westward towards the Shannon callows,
Lusmagh Banagher did sound,
With war cries of the great O'Kelly's,
O'Horan's, and MacCoughlan's ground,
O'Madden there knew hurling joy.

And nowhere did the rowan bloom,
(Ashbuds that take the wind of March),
More grainy than in Kinnitty;
Where MacCoughlan found some room,
With O'Carroll's affinity!
Where O'Delaney still employs.

Kin across the hill in Laois,
Nurturing the ancient art,
(A name that caused our sad decease
Kilkenny's Pat a three goal part,
In '69 with brilliant ploy).

And now we move to Birr's old town,
A stronghold of O'Kennedy,
When he could keep O'Carroll down,
Coolderry way his melody,
Was Brian Boru did wear the crown!

Now if we hand on Galway's breed,
The laurel that great Hector wore,

We bow to what all youngsters need,
A merlin magical to score –
"Johnny - Johnny - Johnny boy!"

Young lad with hurley in your hand,
Don't mind if here your name's not scribed,
Offaly had many septs and clans,
And blood oft comes the female side –
You have good roots my hurling boy.

Town lads used to start with stout ashplant,
To belt a tin can round the yard,
Or street till it was smooth and bland,
(For spiky bits and scant regard),
Till they with friend or foe could toy!

Denis Wrafter (1910 - 1996)

A Sonnet for Johnny Flaherty
(1980 Leinster Hurling Final)

That last goal left no doubt
That genius will win out
In men's affairs.

Sky plucking of that ball
From a back both strong and tall
Dancing Fred Astaire's.

Turn of foot and glide
Swift elusive slide
You had it all!

With what words can versifier
Clinch a hurling flyer?
Artist and great trier.

Of such is genius born
We drank your health till morn!

Denis Wrafter (1910 - 1996)

The Old Man To His Scythe

Old scythe in the hedge,
You're a fright with the rust,
Though myself's little better,
Had I thought of it first!
And to think of the times
And the joys we have known,
When my hone and my stone
Drew a song from your steel;
Such a music we made
In the fields of Ardheel,
When the midges danced jigs
And the sun lavished gold
On the fields of Ardheel -
And the feel of your ash,
And the swish and the flash –
O, barley fell fast
In the fields of Ardheel
Then Mary would come
With a mugful of milk
And a carraway cake –
Such a smoke I would have
Sitting there in the shade,
While my hone and my stone
Put an edge on your blade;
Sitting there in the shade,
I called you my jewel,
And my sweet little tool,
O, the music we made
In the fields of Ardheel!
And to think of you now
Lying down in your rust,
And to think of myself
That's soon to be dust

By The Bog Of Cats

Scene Four

JOSIE *and* MRS KILBRIDE *enter and sit at the garden table as the* CATWOMAN *and* HESTER *exit.*
JOSIE *is dressed: wellingtons, trousers, jumper on inside out. They're playing Snap.*
MRS KILBRIDE *plays ruthlessly, loves to win. JOSIE looks on in dismay.*

MRS K   Snap - snap! Snap! *(Stacking the cards)* How many games is that that I'm after winnin' ya?

JOSIE   Five.

MRS K   And how many did you win?

JOSIE   Ya know right well I won ne'er a game.

MRS K   And do ya know why ya won ne'er a game, Josie? Because you're thick, that's the why.

JOSIE   I always win when I play me Mam.

MRS K   That's only because your Mam is thicker than you. Thick and stubborn and dangerous wrong-headed and backwards to top it all. Are ya goin' to start cryin' now, ya little pussy babby, don't you dare cry, ya need to toughen up, child, what age are ya now? - I says what age are ya?

JOSIE   Seven.

MRS K   Seven auld years. When I was seven I was cookin' dinners for a houseful of men, I was thinnin' turnips twelve hour a day, I was birthin' calves, sowin' corn, stookin' hay, ladin' a bull be his nose, and you can't even win a game of Snap. Sit up straight or ya'll grow up a hunchback. Would ya like that, would ya, to grow up a hunchback? Ya'd be like an auld camel and eveyone'd say, as ya loped by, there goes Josie Kilbride the hunchback, would ya like that, would ya? Answer me.

JOSIE   Ya know right well I wouldn't, Granny.

MRS K   What did I tell ya about callin' me Grandmother.

JOSIE   *(Defiantly)* Granny.

MRS K	*(Leans over the table viciously)* Grandmother! Say it!
JOSIE	*(Giving in)* Grandmother.
MRS K	And you're lucky I even let ya call me that. Ya want another game?
JOSIE	Only if ya don't cheat.
MRS K	When did I cheat?
JOSIE	I seen ya, loads of times.
MRS K	A bad loser's all you are, Josie, and there's nothin' meaner than a had loser. I never cheat. Never. D'ya hear me, do ya? Look me in the eye when I'm talkin' to ya, ya little bastard. D'ya want another game?
JOSIE	No thanks, Grandmother.
MRS K	And why don't ya? Because ya know I'll win, isn't that it? Ya little coward ya, I'll break your spirit yet and then glue ya back the way I want ya. I bet ya can't even spell your name.
JOSIE	And I bet ya I can.
MRS K	G'wan then, spell it.
JOSIE	*(Spells)* J-o-s-i-e K-i-l-b-r- i-d -e.
MRS K	Wrong! Wrong! Wrong!
JOSIE	Well, that's the way Teacher taught me.
MRS K	Are you back-anwerin' me?
JOSIE	No, Grandmother.
MRS K	Ya got some of it right. Ya got the 'Josie' part right, but ya got the 'Kilbride' part wrong, because you're not a Kilbride. You're a Swane. Can ya spell Swane? Of course ya can't. You're Hester Swane's little bastard. You're not a Kilbride and never will be.
JOSIE	I'm tellin' Daddy what ya said.
MRS K	Tell him! Ya won't be tellin' him anythin' I haven't tould him meself. He's an eegit, your Daddy. I warned him about that wan, Hester Swane, that she'd get her claws in, and she did, the tinker. That's what yees are, tinkers. And your poor Daddy, all he's had to put up with. Well, at least that's all changin' now. Why don't yees head off in that auld caravan, back to wherever yees came from, and give your poor Daddy back to me where he rightfully belongs. And you've your jumper on backwards.
JOSIE	It's not backwards, it's inside out.

MRS K   Don't you cheek me - and tell me this, Josie Swane, how much has your Mam in the bank?

JOSIE   I don't know.

MRS K   I'll tell ya how much, a great big goose egg. Useless, that's what she is, livin' off of handouts from my son that she flitters away on whiskey and cigars, the Jezebel witch. *(Smugly)* Guess how much I've saved, Josie, g'wan, guess, guess.

JOSIE   I wish me Mam'd come soon.

MRS K   Ah g'wan, child, guess.

JOS IE   Ten pound.

MRS K   *(Hysterical)* Ten pound! A'ya mad, child? A' ya mad! Ten pound! *(Whispers avariciously)* Three thousand pound. All mine. I saved it. I didn't frig it away on crame buns and blouses. No. I saved it. A thousand for me funeral, a thousand for the Little Sisters of the Poor and a thousand for your Daddy. I'm lavin' you nothin' because your mother would get hould of it. And d'ya think would I get any thanks for savin' all that money? Oh no, none, none in the world. Would it ever occur to anywan to say, well done, Mrs Kilbride, well done, Elsie, not wance did your Daddy ever say, well done, Mother, no, too busy fornicatin' with Hester Swane, too busy bringin' little bastards like yourself into the world.

JOSIE   Can I go and play now?

MRS K   Here, I brung ya sweets, g'wan ate them, ate them all, there's a great child, ya need some sugar, some sweetie pie sweetness in your life. C'mere and give your auld Grandmother a kiss. *(JOSIE does)* Sure it's not your fault ya were born a little girl bastard. D'ya want another game of Snap? I'll let ya win.

JOSIE   No.

MRSK   Don't you worry, child, we'll get ya off of her yet. Me and your Daddy has plans. We'll batter ya into the semblance of legitimacy yet, soon as we get ya off-

Enter CARTHAGE

CARTHAGE   I don't know how many times I tould ya to lave the child alone. You've her poisoned with your bile and rage.

MRS K   I'm sayin' nothin' that isn't true. Can't I play a game of

	Snap with me own granddaughter?
CARTHAGE	Ya know I don't want ya around here at the minute. G' wan home, Mother, g'wan.
MRS K	And do what? Talk to the range? Growl at God?
CARTHAGE	Do whatever ya like, only lave Josie alone, pick on somewan your own size. *(Turning JOSIE'S jumper the right way around)* You'll have to learn to dress yourself.
MRS K	Ah now, Carthage, don't be annoyed with me. I only came up to say goodbye to her, found her in her pyjamas out here playin' in the snow. Why isn't her mother mindin' her?
CARTHAGE	Don't start in on that again.
MRS K	I never left you on your own.
CARTHAGE	Ya should have.
MRS K	An ya never called into see the new dress I got for today and ya promised ya would. (CARTHAGE *glares at her)* Alright, I'm goin', I'm goin. Just don't think now ya've got Caroline Cassidy ya can do away with me, the same as you're doin' away with Hester Swane. I'm your mother and I won't be goin' away. Ever.

And exit MRS KILBRIDE

CARTHAGE	Where's your Mam?
JOSIE	Isn't she always on the bog? Can I go to your weddin'?
CARTHAGE	What does your mother say?
JOSIE	She says there'll be no weddin' and to stop annoyin' her.
CARTHAGE	Does she now?
JOSIE	Will you ax her for me?
CARTHAGE	We'll see, Josie, we'll see.
JOSIE	I'll wear me Communion dress. Remember me Communion, Daddy?
CARTHAGE	I do.
JOSIE	Wasn't it just a brilliant day?
CARTAGE	It was, sweetheart, it was. Come on we'll go check the calves.

And exit the pair.

Rita Kelly

Droichead na Sionainne

Mám soilse i lár na hiargúltachta,
b'shin an tsibhialtacht dúinne
ón taobh eile den tSionainn
ó réimsí leathan féir is portach -
Rachra, cathair faoi dhraíocht dúinn.

Do shín is do shín sruth na Sionainne
amach is amach ós ár gcomhar
go dtí go raibh
an tSráidbhaile mar líne tithe,
is soilse spréite ar dhroim an domhain.

D'fhan raidhse an tsamhraidh go léir
faoi thoinn, boladh blasta
an *meadowsweet* -
ní bhacamar riamh lena ainm oifigiúl:
'airgead luachra'.

Chualamar slopaireacht slim na taoide
ar na céimeanna aolchloiche
ar chúl an tí ....tír álainn trína chéile ...
bhí céimeanna mar sin ag gach teach
agus bhí gach teach ina bhád
bunoscionn
David Copperfield muidine go léir is Betsy Trotwood
i bhfad uainn, b'fhéidir.
Nach rabhamar i lár cruinne cosúil chuile dhuine
ina n-áit féin.

Bhí an spéir is na réalta go léir ar foluain fúinn.
Iad ar fad casta bunoscionn sna tuiltí abhann.

Rita Kelly

Traein na Tulaí Móire

Ní bhionn fhios againn
cá dtitfidh an scéal
nó cén chúinne den domhan
ina mbeidhimid nuair a bhrisfidh
an nóiméad.

Bhí mé féin i nDún Éidean, ó thuaidh, i gcéin,
plódaithe le héigse is fuisce is olagón na bpíob
i bpríomhchathair na hOchtú Aoise Dhéag,
Boswell agus criticí na n-irisí liteartha
ina scuaine taibhsiúil sna cearnóga
ina bhfuil smúit na gcianta ar a n-aghaidheanna.
Ní liom carraig bhuan Dhún Eidean ná ní liom
dreach dúr an Domhnaigh, ná foisceart na Banríona
i racht goil, i muinín a croí.
Is fada uaim an t-achar, Banríon ag cailliúint a cinn
in aduaineas Londan.

Tháinig an drochscéal ar maidin,
táim anois ar traein na Tulaí Móire
ag sní isteach is amach idir na n-eascrach.
Rachaidh an traein amach go Clara -
áit ina raibh m'athairse óg tráth.
Áit is am go mba fhada uaidh
lomfhuacht an bháis.
Ritheann an traein ar aghaidh agus sonann na logainmeacha
atá sáite sa chuimhne ar aon dul leis an roth iarainn
á chíorclú féin ar mhíneadas an iarainnróid.
Téim siar, siar arís, sa tslí chéanna ina ndeachaigh sé fhéin siar
chomh minic sin sul má bhí mé fhéin fiú i gcrot na mBeo.
Inniu, tá sé dulta siar is a aghaidh dúnta
i gcrot na Marbh.

Rita Kelly

Na boird - Móna is Soláthar Leictreachais

B'ionadh dúinn riamh móin á meilt acu
agus smúdar móna á dtarraingt acu
i gcarráistí beaga bréagánacha
go craos mór an tStáisiúin.

B'ionadh dúinn, lá grianghaofar samhraidh,
lá liathchorcra lár na bliana
cneas an phortaigh briste agus tarraingthe siar acu
is leathanacht nach bhfuil insint air
ag síneadh uainn amach
go ciúnas Chluain Mhic Nóis.

B'ionadh dúinn
na carráistí buídathacha
ag rith ar úrlár mín an phortaigh,
is na milliúin duillí tite á mhuscailt acu
as suan codlata na cianta.

Fuinneamh as cuimse, faoi cheilt
i bportach lár na tíre
agus bhíomar ag croílár na cumhachta
ag seoladh solais is fuinnimh
do gach cistin is cúinne
chomh fada sin uainn:-
go háiteanna bríomhaire
go mBailtí Móra is cathracha nua aoiseacha
ina raibh borradh faoi gach ní...

seachas suaimhneas seanda
na gcrann is na nduilleog
i ndoimhneacht dhubh Ua bhFáilí

Rita Kelly

Bádóireacht

Maidin shamhraidh, roimh guth ar ghéag,
roimh briseadh ar bith ar an mbríonglóid -
cos amach ar adhmad an urláir go faiteach.
Mé mar gadaí ar fud an tí, ag éalú chun an tsrutha.

Céimeanna beaga bideacha trí na garraithe.
Drúcht drisiúil seancharracha néantógacha
is bábógaí briste.
An ghrian ag smaoineamh air i rosamh na spéire,
ag marcaíocht go ciúin, aclaí
ar chuisle na huiscí: an bád.

An eochair faoi cheilt, faoi chloch.
Tommy Coleman, ba leis an bád aerach seo,
bhí 'deal' déanta againn:
cead agam é a úsáid am ar bith roimh a sé ar maidin
in ainneoin is in aineolas mo thuismí
iad fós sáite i limistéar na súile dúnta.

Amach liom ag ramhaíocht.
An bád a shlíobadh féin
ar airgead na maidine.
Is na braoiníní beaga ag sileadh go soilseach
solasmhar ó bhrúsa an maide ramha.

Do bhris mé caoi isteach in aghaidh, i ndromchla is i ndreach
na Sionainne
is do bhris mistéir is miotaseolaíocht mhór
na mochmhaidine isteach orm
faoi na dTrí hÁirsí Déag.

James Scully

Potato Picking

Waiting: Warm within. Doubly insulated, maternal wrappings and fried bread. Fraternal frolics greeting the school-free day.

Bumping: The grey Ferguson, perilous open-backed trailer drew us like Reformatory Boys to a distant workplace.

Arriving: Crows cawing, hoary landscape, detritus filled avenue, soft verges scarred by solid tyres.

Preparing: Eskerside fields, sacks, buckets, a machine, apprehension, "Uncle" Mick exhaling frost and smoke. Simultaneous combustion.

Picking: Hands inexplicably warmed by frozen clay. Legs wellie-rimmed. The spuddler remorselessly anticipating each drill's end.
To hand, to bucket, to sack, to trailer, to pit, to pot, to plate, to pit, to earth.

Earning: Short day, limited mid-winter light. Paytime, sweaty-palmed flushes awaiting bounty. 10/= note. The lurid Lady Lavery.

Homecoming: Triumphant wage earner, a day's work done, first time contributor to Christmas. The myth of Santa Claus unfurled. Solstice signalled.

James Scully

August 1998

Did it ever occur to you that John Troy was the Van Gogh of hurling?

The ruddish complexion, receding temple, high cheekbone;
modesty to a fault, self-deprecating
(Those earnest acknowledgements of colleague assists.)

Tormented by a Provencal sun,
Helmeted like the bandaged Van Gogh,
Laden with instinctive talent,
an artist, the master of his oeuvre.

Gifted hand to eye co-ordination
Deft flicks, flecks, feints, swirls, twirls
Fuelling redolent memories
For All-Starry nights.

Offaly's titles are all in colour
befitting Van Troys luminous palette.

Strutting the sun drenched summertime landscapes
Creating vivid masterpieces
Where dimensions are evident only in retrospect.

The master craftsman, surreal impressionist,
Burning intensely on the Croker canvas or Semple Fidelis

Patrick Carton

Iona

Who dwells in dreams of diamonds
and strays on ways of stone
who milks the might of many
and always goes alone
who sees the sparks flying from the fire
bring tear-drops from the skies
who lingers in the house of love
in solitary guise
who trembles on the threshold
and follows fleeting flags
who strides by shining street-lamps
and crawls on crooked crags
who glories in his granite
to make his magic mud
who wants to walk on water
bears the boots of blood
whose injury is innocence
who calls his profit pain
who asks the arms of Adam
to make the mark of Cain
who charts a stormy sea-way
beneath a broken sky
to the island of Iona
to hear the white dove cry.

Joe Conlon

Sparrow Hawk

Laser eyes
In sea-blue skies,
Goodbyes
On the wings.
You dance my dream,
Then that thrusted
Plunge, a scream,
My dream
On broken wings.

Joe Conlon

How The Hay Was Saved
(for the triumphant Offaly Hurling Team '98)

The same story
The same four walls
Defeating us,
Black days, bleak nights,
Catch the rain
With your mouth open.
The flow of the summer
Bursting its banks everywhere.
Fields, bogs pale shadows,
These uncatchable crops.
Another year in exility's chains.
Say a prayer, for God's sake!
We did it. It happened!
The tricolour of our dreams
Coming up with flying colours.
Now we have something
To look back on.
Something to look forward to
Fodder for the Winter
Food for thought.

Joe Conlon

Pitchforks To The Sky
(for Jimmy Hanley)

Out of reach now,
The simplicity of a life
Now complicated by
The wheels
Of robotic motion.
Pitchforks to the sky
Throw me back decades,
Battlefields of haste,
The race against time.
You're in shirt sleeves
Making hay under oceanic skies.
You are one of the fleet,
A sail in the wind
Coming to our rescue,
Your frail figure towering
Above us as you hoist
The withered grass
Onto the climbing cocks
Of a July evening,
We scale the heights
Of your labours, the quick
Little hills of Everest
Are our playground now.
We slide to the ground,
We run on unscathed
By the thrust of fall,
We play hide and go seek,
We are children
In fields forever,
Sipping the champagne
Of laughter
Sipping the last
of your summer wine.

Donny Clavin, the Real Seanchaí

Joe Conlon

I Left The Door Open

Ever since I became a bachelor
When my whole family
Deserted me for somebody else,
I left the door open,
Hoping against all hope,
That you would walk
Across the threshold
And close it.

Biographical Notes

Joe Kenny was born in Mayo, but has lived most of his life in Tullamore and taught in Tullamore Vocational School until his retirement. He has had several plays broadcast on Radio Eireann and an extract from one was featured in a Niall Toibin one-man show at the Gaiety Theatre. He has recently begun to write again with the encouragement of Tullamore Writers' Group.

Connie Roberts was born in Tullamore in 1962, one of fifteen children . From the age of four she lived in an orphanage - Mount Carmel in Moate, County Westmeath. From the age of eight onwards, her home-away-from-home was a foster family in Tullamore. She now lives in New York.

Phil Robinson has lived all her married life near Kinnitty, Birr, County Offaly with her husband Tony and family. Phil has been writing poetry for five years and has been a regular contributor to the Midland Tribune and has had six of her poems published by Arrival Press in Peterborough.

Eugene Sweeney resides in Mullingar. His family originally came from Tullamore. He is a painter and decorator and has been writing poetry for about ten years. He has previously had work published by the International Library of Poetry and the International Society of Poets.

Teresa Kelly is from Ballycumber and studied nutrition in Dublin. She lived in Northern Ireland for a number of years and is now based in Galway. She has written poetry for the last five years and has previously read at Poets Platform in Cúirt.

Maureen Lowndes lives in Geashill, County Offaly. She has one teenage son. Her work has previously been published in the Laois Anthology and a book published by the Diocesan Pastoral Council in Carlow College.

Derek Fanning was born in Ballinasloe, County Galway in February 1971 and grew up in Birr, County Offaly. He was educated in Birr National School, Stonyhurst College, Lancashire England and De Montfort

University, Leicester, England. Since leaving De Montfort University in 1993, he has lived and worked in Birr and currently works as a journalist for the "Midland Tribune", which is based in the South Offaly town.

Tom Murray was born in Ballinvalley, Killeigh, County Offaly in 1927. He grew up with three brothers and two sisters on his parents' farm. He worked as Field Sales Manager for a large paper company until he retired in 1992. He has written a 60,000 word manuscript about growing up on a farm in the Midlands in the late 1930's and is currently in the process of publishing same.

Michael Dongean was born in 1953 and is a teacher in Rath National School, Birr, County Offaly. He is very interested in community theatre and has written and directed various pieces for performances. He is married with three children.

Mary Dunne was born and educated in Tullamore. At an early age she developed a keen interest in all aspects of the theatre. She is a founder member and now Honorary Life-President of the Tullamore Amateur Dramatic Society. Photographer by trade, she also runs the "Act One Scene Two" Youth Drama Group.

Vera Hughes is from County Sligo, but has lived in Moate since 1956. In 1988 she wrote and published 'The Strange Story of Sarah Kelly", a factual account of a 19th Century English landlord in the Midlands. A second edition was published in 1998. Vera has had poems, stories and articles published in various magazines and was winner of the Clovendale Prize for Irish poetry (in English) for 1993. She is a member of both Athlone and Tullamore Writers' Groups.

Dr. Alec Hughes was born in Dublin and came to Moate in 1954 where he practised as a G. P. for over forty years. Among his many interests was writing, especially poetry, and several of his poems appeared in various publications. His sudden death in November, 1998 shocked the whole community, especially fellow members in Tullamore and Athlone Writers' Groups. Ar dheis Dé go raibh a anam uasal caoih!

Brid Broderick was born in Tullamore in 1955. She holds an MSc in Biomedical Sciences and is senior in charge of the Biochemistry Department in the General Hospital, Tullamore. She has been a member of the Offaly Community Arts Group since 1989 and her interests include all areas of the arts. She has exhibited paintings in a number of exhibitions in Offaly.

Carol Burke was born in Tullamore and has lived there all her life. She is married to Aidan and has one child, Emma. She works as Clinic Secretary with the Sisters of Charity of Jesus and Mary.

Maureen Comerford lives in Tullamore and is a housewife who works part time for Dúchas.

Fiona McKeown is twelve years old and from Clara. She is a first year student in Ard Scoil Chiarain in Clara.

Ann Egan is a poet and historian from the borders of counties Laois and Offaly. She now lives in Kildare, where she is currently Writer in Schools. She has won the Listowel Writers' Week poetry prize three times and many other awards. Her poetry is widely published including 'The Darkness Echoing" R.T. E. Radio One.

Sean O'Connor is a native of Clara, County Offaly. Born in 1948, he received his education in the local Franciscan School and Clara Vocational School. He sat his Leaving Certificate as a mature student with V.T.O S. in 1994. He is married with six children.

Paul Egan was born in 1969 and resided in Rath until recently when he moved to Dovehill in Kilcormac. He was educated in St. John's National School, Rath and Kilcormac Vocational School. He qualified as a cabinetmaker/joiner in 1990. He was unfortunate to encounter bad health in 1991 when he was diagnosed as having M.E. Fortunately his health has improved quite spectacularly and he now paints as an artist and is also involved in the field of complementary medicine.

Georgina Brennan is a native of Portlaoise, County Laois. She has been living in Tullamore since 1985. She is married and has two children. She is a member of Tullamore Writers' Group and is, at present working on her first novel.

Geraldine Brosnahan is a founding member of the Offaly Writers Group. She moved from Scotland to Ireland five years ago and now lives in Daingean. She has been writing for six years and has had a number of short stories published. She has also won two writing awards, The Offaly/Leinster Express Short Story Competition and the Bill Naughton Award in Ballyhaunis, County Mayo. Geraldine is currently working on a novel which is based in the Irish Midlands and Manchester. She divides her time between her teaching career and writing.

Michael Egan was born in 1963 and comes from a farming background. He left school at the age of fifteen and trained as a carpenter. Over the next fifteen years he continued to educate himself. He is very interested in meditation. He has written a booklet which he titled "Time to Change" based on how he thought that the economy and society in general could he improved. He is currently writing his autobiography.

Eileen Casey (ncc Cordial) is a native of Birr, County Offaly and has lived in Dublin for several years now. Her work has been widely published in magazines, journals and anthologies. She has won various awards for her work. The awards include the Moore Medallion, and the A I.B./Western People Poetry prize. Currently she is creative writing tutor with Dublin V.E.C. and Ashfield College, Templeogue.

Jim Brennan lives in Daingean, County Offaly. His first collection of poetry "Over the High Bank" was recently published by Tympanum Publications.

El Biffo is a teacher in Killina Secondary School in Rahan.

Jackie Gorman is twenty seven years old and is a native of Athlone, but has lived in Banagher for several years. She is currently doing development work in the Gambia, West Africa and hopes to return to Offaly in 2001.

Carol Kavanagh is 13 years old and comes from Ferbane. She is interested in writing and hopes to continue writing through her growing years.

Ber Brophy comes from Clara and is now living in Tullamore. She is a housewife with six children who has recently started to write poetry.

Aisling English is twenty two years old and is a native of Tullamore. She trained as a nurse in St. James' hospital and is currently working in Tullamore Hospital.

Ann Tyrell-McCormack was born in Tullamore and has lived there all her life. She has two sons and three daughters and she runs her own business.

Denis Wrafter was born in Ballyduff in 1910. He was educated at St Columba's C.B.S. Tullamore. He was employed as Clerical Officer with Offaly County Council for 41 years. He took up duty on the 1st of July, 1927 and retired on the 6th of August, 1968. His poetry was published in two anthologies "New Irish Poets, New York"; Devin Adair 1947 and "1000 Years of Irish Poetry" also published by Devin Adair in 1947. His poems were also published in the Irish Times and in the local press. He was a skilled sportsman and had a keen interest in hurling. A number of his poems reflect this interest and love of the game and the skills of the players.

Marina Carr was born in 1964 and grew up in County Offaly. She graduated from University College Dublin in 1987. Her early plays include "Low in the Dark", "The Deer's Surrender", "This Love Thing", "Ullaloo", "The Mai" and "Portia Coughlan". Marina currently lives in Dublin with her family. She has been Writer-in-Association at the Abbey and is a member of Aosdana. She is currently Writer-in-Residence at Trinity College.

Rita Kelly was born in Galway in 1953 and grew up in mid and east Galway. She lived in Shannonbridge in the early 60's when there was still a one-teacher school there. Though her father was a native of Ballinasloe, he was taken to Clara by his aunt Margaret Clyne, when his mother died, and was reared there. She writes in Irish and English - poetry, fiction, drama and criticism. She is Writer-in-Residence for Laois County Council.

James Scully is a teacher in the primary school in Banagher.

Patrick Carton is from Horseleap and is currently studying in Galway.

Joe Conlon is a farmer from Edenderry. His first collection "Fields of Evening" was recently published by Topic Newspapers.